"...Like a Stone Wall"

Gen. Thomas J. "Stonewall" Jackson, CSA

by

Robert K. Krick

Published 1997
Farnsworth Military Impressions
401 Baltimore Street
Gettysburg, PA 17325
(717) 334-8838

Cover Photo: Library of Congress

ISBN: 0-9643632-8-3

DEDICATION

For the regal BJK,
to whom stonewalling is a way of life.

INTRODUCTION

No American soldier has ever grasped the popular imagination more thoroughly, and held it more tenaciously, than the quiet, determined man from Virginia's western mountains who came to be called "Stonewall." The riveting story of Thomas J. Jackson took a grip on me in my nonage. Growing up near the Sierra Nevada—not the Blue Ridge—and unencumbered by Confederate ancestry or Southern propinquity, I came across Stonewall's traces in books and was fascinated. The dour, pious, deadly efficient general has affected each of many generations of his countrymen in much the same fashion, and is likely to continue his impact on the imagination of Americans yet unborn.

A vast literature exists on the life and attainments of Stonewall Jackson. The majority of it is sloppy, inaccurate, even downright silly. Books purely derivative, without an iota of new evidence or a hint of new insight, appear steadily. Some splendid biographies stand above the plebeian flood: G.F.R. Henderson's classic military study; Lenoir Chambers' thorough, two-volume work; James I. Robertson's large new book, based on fresh research; and Frank Vandiver's gorgeously written biography (the best single starting point for Jackson).

In the face of the extant body of writing about Jackson, why undertake another biographical sketch, and a notably short one at that? This brief treatise does contain heretofore unpublished information, but that is only interesting grist. My main purpose is to interpret in an accessible format the well-known facts about one of the towering figures in American military history.

Preparing a book of these dimensions on a subject so familiar of course involved virtually no new research. Instead it employed encyclopaedic files accumulated over several decades. The historians who contributed pieces to those files are precisely the same folks, known to everyone working on eastern-theater Confederate topics, who cheerfully vector historical material great and small to their colleagues who are specializing in various subjects. Foremost among them in my case is Robert E. L. Krick, as well as Keith S. Bohannon, Gary W. Gallagher, Graham Dozier, Michael P. Musick, Stephen L. Ritchie, John R. P. Bass, Lowell Reidenbaugh, Barbara Moore, Peter S. Carmichael, Michael A. Lynn, Noel

G. Harrison, Francis A. O'Reilly, Mac Wyckoff, Richard J. Sommers, Donald C. Pfanz, Ben Ritter, John P. Ackerly III, Bruce Allardice, Russell Bailey, Zack C. Waters, Kirk Denkler, Rob Hodge, Clark B. Hall, George Skoch, Lawrence T. Jones, T. Michael Parrish, Thomas P. and Bev Lowry, Dana MacBean, Jim McLean, Mike Taylor, Mike Masters, Lee A. Wallace, Jr., Jack Bales, Suzanne Christoff, Glenn L. McMullen, Mike Miller, William J. Miller, Robert G. Tanner, Diane Jacob, and Keith E. Gibson.

Robert K. Krick
Fredericksburg, Virginia

PIETY, PROBITY, AND IMPRACTICALITY

By the time Thomas Jackson reached his assignment at primitive Fort Meade, Florida, in 1850, he was a West Point graduate and a combat veteran seasoned by hard fighting in the Mexican War. Battlefield prowess had won Jackson the brevet rank of major. He was, however, still only twenty-six years old. The relative inexperience of youth, combined with a dawning religious awareness and a life-long sternness about rectitude, would turn Jackson's assignment in Florida into an ugly nightmare.

Jackson's ascetic nature doubtless faced fewer disappointments at the listless frontier post than those that afflicted most of the fort's other inhabitants. Some early scouting assignments, including a 90-mile march in three days, occupied the major for a time. Eventually the absence of any meaningful duty bored most of Fort Meade's garrison; it gave Jackson too much time to worry about, perhaps imagine, moral turpitude in others. The perceived depravity cropped up in the worst possible place—in the behavior of William H. French, who happened to be Jackson's immediate superior and the post's commander.

French also held a brevet majority, but he enjoyed seniority held by a narrow margin. The two men fell out over interpretation of Jackson's collateral duties as post quartermaster. The district commander gave Quartermaster Jackson's tedious arguments in the matter no credence, and said so firmly in writing. Soon thereafter the differences between the two majors exploded when Jackson heard talk among the fort's enlisted men and servants about alleged improper behavior between French (whose pregnant wife was living on the post) and a servant girl.

The confused, seamy business was not susceptible to ready understanding in 1851, and the passage of nearly a century and a half has further beclouded the issues. Looking at the record prompts a modern historian to the same conclusion that the contestants' superiors reached long ago: both men ought to cease and desist, and move on to something else. They did: French, adjudged "incapable of conducting...a detached post," to other duty; Jackson, in a crucial decision that affected his life dramatically, to leave the army and teach at the twelve-year-old military academy in Lexington, Virginia.

ORPHANED AND UNTUTORED

Nothing in Tom Jackson's breeding or early youth suggested the inculcation of the kind of inflexible fiber he demonstrated in Florida and thereafter. Thomas Jonathan Jackson was born in Clarksburg, (West) Virginia, on January 21, 1824, the son of Julia Beckwith Neale and Jonathan Jackson. The father, an improvident lawyer, died a few weeks after Tom's second birthday. Julia remarried four years later and died not long thereafter. Orphaned at seven, Tom spent the next decade as the ward of kinfolk. Chief among them was Uncle Cummins E. Jackson, a large, self-reliant man of considerable energy who operated Jackson's Mill, near Weston. Cummins and the other Jacksons treated their young relative well. Some modern writers have wrung their hands over poor Tom Jackson's childhood, and postulated preposterously that it foreordained him to be a gloomy, religious, inflexible adult. There is nothing in the record—barring the death of his parents—that supplies strong support for such a convenient, romantic oversimplification.

Formal education was not in ready supply in the mountain country. Tom Jackson benefitted from only intermittent schooling and tutoring. He absorbed enough to become a teacher himself for four months in 1840-41, in a five-pupil log-cabin school. His Uncle Cummins suffered through an extended legal probe concerning financial irregularities, but retained enough standing to help Tom win a post as constable when he was seventeen. The wide experience that the youngster acquired in that duty expanded his horizons and made him into a skilled, albeit graceless, horseman. Although the invigorating frontier environment of Jackson's youth no doubt conditioned him for a life full of challenges, it was far from the ideal preparation for one destined to attend the United States Military Academy at West Point—an institution immodestly, but not inaptly, styled "The Best School in the World" by its proponents. A curriculum heavy on mathematics and scientific subjects bore little relation to the schooling Thomas had known in his backwoods milieu.

A RUSTIC AT WEST POINT

Tom Jackson arrived at West Point, classmate George B. McClellan remembered, "an awkward, bashful boy...with the worst sort of preparation [but] his pluck was absolutely marvelous." The man who had commanded the Army of the Potomac in 1861 and 1862 concluded with hindsight that classmate Jackson clearly "deserved success and fame" on the basis of "almost superhuman work," the product of the Virginian's astonishing determination. Federal General Henry J. Hunt was among many others who eschewed hindsight in describing Cadet Jackson. Hunt admitted, "never was a man more surprized than I was at the mark he made."

Everyone who watched the ill-trained young man master the academic rigors of the Military Academy remarked upon his tenacity. On June 19, 1842, when Jackson arrived to take the entrance examination, his scholastic future was far from certain. Congressman Samuel L. Hays, who played the central role in securing the appointment, carefully described Jackson's potential as based less on actual achievements than on "an improvable mind" and a record of relying "entirely on his own exertions." On the afternoon of June 25 the Academic Board announced the names of candidates found qualified for admission. Thomas J. Jackson's was the last name on the list.

"The life of a cadet," one of Jackson's contemporaries wrote, "is one of extreme monotony." Precisely such a disciplined environment suited Jackson's developmental needs. He thrived at the Academy. Despite his imperfect educational basis, Tom managed to finish 45th in mathematics among his first-year class of 83 cadets, and 51st overall. In conduct—which the Academy calculated across all four classes—Jackson stood 38th in a corps that numbered 223. The next year he improved to 30th of 78 class members (18th in mathematics but only 68th in drawing, as his jagged, awkward penmanship would attest). One senior cadet who helped Jackson grapple with his studies was W. H. C. Whiting, who during the Civil War would come to loathe his quondam protege. The improvement continued to 20th in the school year ending in June 1845, including an 11th in philosophy; and in conduct, Tom Jackson stood first in the entire corps. The next year a stellar showing in Ethics helped pull Jackson to 17th rank in the graduating class.

The rustic youth who mastered a scholastic overload did not at the same time develop the relaxed social poise that came naturally to most other cadets. John Gibbon, later a Union general, described Jackson as "a tall, raw-boned young man...exceedingly shy and bashful....the most diffident of men." In the presence of a complimentary superior officer soon after graduation, Gibbon wrote, Jackson "blushed like a girl & stood confused before the company."

Tom Jackson and his roommate George Stoneman, another Federal general in training, were both so quiet that next-door neighbor John C. Tidball (destined to be a distinguished Yankee artillery chief) "scarcely knew they were there." Tidball expressed amazement at Jackson's "ex-

CADET "STONEWALL" JACKSON.

cessive diffidence." He also described Tom's "somewhat shambling, awkward gait and the habit of carrying his head down in a thoughtful attitude," and a voice "thin and feminine, almost squeaky, while his utterances were quick, jerky, and sententious." Tidball adroitly summarized Jackson as reminding him of a Biblical figure said to be "like unto a cake unturned."

The woodenly uncertain young man, full of determination and rectitude, frequently behaved in a manner that looked silly to his mates. One recalled "time and again" seeing Jackson do such things as "march solemnly at the usual pace, deviating neither to the right nor the left" after everyone else in a cadet parade had raced for shelter from a cloudburst. Egbert Viele—yet another Union general-to-be—illustrated Jackson's "wonderful conscientiousness" with a story about a night when the two cadets were on adjacent guard posts. Beyond them was another post assigned to a "devil-may-care" first-class officer named Wood who ordered Jackson to keep an eye peeled for the officer of the day, while he took a nap in the sentry box. Jackson undertook this somewhat illicit chore (it was an order after all) by perching in a painful posture on a stool to make sure he remained awake and alert.

Obeying a marginally spurious order was one thing; accepting random misbehavior quite another. Cadet Jackson revealed the rigid expectations that later would be so familiar to his Confederate subordinates in the way he reacted to a petty episode of Academy life. A lazy cadet took Jackson's musket (scrupulously maintained, of course) and substituted his own to avoid the drudgery of cleaning it. The imposed-upon Virginian told his officers of the switch, one of his best friends recalled, and alerted them to watch for his secret marks on the weapon at the forthcoming inspection. When the culprit was uncovered, Jackson's "rage became almost uncontrollable," according to his close friend William E. Jones. "The petty theft, prompted only by laziness," Jones remarked, "seemed to [Jackson to] show a moral depravity disgracing to humanity." Only with difficulty did the faculty restrain Jackson from pressing formal charges all the way to the War Department. (Jackson's evaluation of the miscreant was accurate, events showed. The fellow was expelled from West Point for sordid moral misdeeds [did this affect Jackson's later view of Major French and the servant girl?], and took up an outlaw career in the West that included murder in its catalogue of infamies.)

MEXICO

A few weeks before Thomas J. Jackson graduated from the Military Academy and donned the insignia of a second lieutenant in the United States Army, Americans and Mexicans began fighting in disputed border country near the Rio Grande. In July 1846, Congress declared war. Lieutenant Jackson soon found himself in its midst as a subaltern in a battery of horse-drawn "flying artillery." Service with the guns suited the new lieutenant. He reached Monterrey, Mexico, in late November, joining Ulysses Grant, Cadmus Wilcox, and several other West Point contemporaries there. The battery then formed part of General Winfield Scott's expeditionary force that landed at Vera Cruz in March 1847 and moved on Mexico City in a masterfully managed campaign.

Jackson's careful attention to duty around Vera Cruz and his nonchalant bravery under fire won him mention in dispatches, and brevet promotion to first lieutenant. The battery had little opportunity for distinction at Cerro Gordo, but the lieutenant's battery commander lauded Jackson's "great exertions" in what Jackson proudly described as "very flattering terms." Chagrin, even "mortification," followed on the heels of Cerro Gordo: Jackson received orders to remain behind the primary column in a garrison post. He used the leisure to study Spanish and even, in an atypical burst for one so acutely shy, contemplated "making some lady acquaintances...."

General Scott's desire to have ample artillery at hand for storming Mexico City gave Lieutenant Jackson the opportunity for which he had been yearning. His "excessive ambition," Jackson admitted, made him eager "to be near the enemy in the fight." On August 19 at Contreras and Churubusco he got his wish. Not only did the lieutenant discharge his own duties in "handsome style," his commander wrote, but he also filled in for a slain senior lieutenant in "equally conspicuous" fashion. The official report concluded enthusiastically: "I cannot too highly recommend [Jackson] to the major general's favorable consideration." The favorable consideration gained a brevet to captain for the ambitious young artillerist.

Nothing he had yet accomplished compared to Captain Jackson's ordeal on September 13 and the triumphant success that followed. While infantry stormed dramatically against the Mexican citadel atop Chapultepec Hill, Jackson pushed a section of artillery toward the capital city, farther to the front than anyone had thought he could go. Enemy fire whistled through the guns, hitting horses and men and driving the survivors into deep road-side ditches. At least one artillery round zipped between the brevet captain's legs. Jackson remained erect and alone on the fire-swept surface, shouting "There's no danger....I am not hit!" He finally coaxed a sergeant out of the ditch and the two men put one gun into action. When the tide turned in favor of the Americans, Jackson stayed far forward, repulsing two mounted charges against his exposed position. He later described being "in a road which was swept with grape and canister, and at the same time thousands of muskets from the castle itself above pouring down like hail...." His battery commander wrote of Jackson's "devotion, industry, talent, and gallantry." His division commander applauded Jackson as "brave...did invaluable service." Another division commander's official report took the unusual step of referring to Jackson, who was entirely outside his organization, with such words as "chivalrously," "gallant," and "noble courage." Even commander-in-chief Scott mentioned Jackson twice in his official report. The events of September 13 won yet another brevet promotion, to major. Fourteen years later Thomas Jackson would still proudly bear the hard-earned title of Major Jackson as he began a career on the far wider stage of the American Civil War.

With all of Mexico won by Scott's army (abetted by Jackson's much-praised section of artillery), occupation of the conquered land became the assigned duty. Unlike many of his compatriots, Major Jackson was much taken with Mexico, Mexicans, the culture, and the language. He bought a fine horse, learned to dance and then did so often, studied Spanish, and explored Catholic beliefs. He even entertained the hedonistic notion of remaining in Mexico City, where he found "mirth, beauty, fine manners, variety, and in fine all that man can reasonably want." After nine months of such fanciful pastimes, interspersed with military occupation duties, Jackson returned home and was posted to a quiet peace-time station at Fort Hamilton in New York harbor.

The major's two years in New York afforded little opportunity for distinction, advancement, or growth as an officer. He studiously took the time to advance as a man, however, launching a strict regimen of private reading and self-improvement. "I propose...to be a hard student," he declared with characteristic determination. Unfortunately, none of that earnest endeavor prepared Thomas Jackson for the knotty problems awaiting him in Florida.

A PROFESSORIAL MEDIOCRITY

What would have become of Major Jackson's career in the U. S. Army after his ugly tilt with Major French in Florida in 1851 is difficult to imagine. Luckily he did not face that unhappy prospect. He found instead a delightful—and much-needed—mix of contentment, love, and intellectual stimulation while living in Lexington, Virginia, and professing at the Virginia Military Institute. The 1850's prepared T. J. Jackson to become "Stonewall" during the 1860's.

Jackson's appointment at so fortuitous a time came about as a result of two fateful coincidences: earlier candidates for the VMI post fell by the wayside; and Daniel Harvey Hill happened to remember Jackson from a chance 1846 encounter and mentioned him when VMI's superintendent asked about good candidates. Hill later became Jackson's brother-in-law and a Confederate major general, but his role in this pivotal 1851 episode was purely happenstance.

Major Jackson's chair was as "Professor of Natural and Experimental Philosophy and Artillery Tactics." He came to the Institute wonderfully well equipped to instruct artillery tactics, but the scientific curriculum—mostly what today would be called physics—posed an immense challenge. By the stern application that Jackson always applied to any problem, he came to grips with the necessary subject matter. He never did, however, master even the most rudimentary techniques of public speaking. For almost ten years after he reported to VMI on August 13, 1851, Major Jackson bored, amused, or enraged teenagers obliged to learn in his section room. The cadets' chagrin gave vent to complaints both informal and formal. Bits of amateur doggerel damned "such a *hell of a fool*, whose name is Jackson" and grumbled about "Major Jackson, Hell & Thunder!"
Midway through his decade in Lexington, Jackson faced an attack on his classroom performance far more significant than any youthful poesy. Word of deficiencies in Jackson's teaching techniques had reached the Institute's influential alumni society and prompted a request for a review by the Board of Visitors. The Board tabled the request (when Jackson learned of the matter much later, he characteristically demanded—in vain—a formal hearing). The Board probably was influenced to quiescence by the superintendent, who later conceded that Professor Jackson "was not a success....He was no *teacher*, and he lacked the tact required in getting along with his classes." Jackson's superior hastened to add, however, that Jackson, the Mexican War hero, was widely respected as "brave... conscientious...and a good man, but he was no professor...."

Fortunately, Jackson's battlefield achievements buttressed his reputation among both the cadets suffering through his classes and the faculty skeptics. "He has the reputation of being one of the best artillerists in the service," the Institute's superintendent wrote proudly. On the drill field the awkward pedagogue of the physics lab turned comfortably, happily into a seasoned gunnery instructor. Despite inadequate equipment, Artillerist Jackson made the parade ground into a solid training facility. He requisitioned horses from other departments to pull the guns, or simply designated a crew of cadets to drag the pieces around as human draught horses. Cadets undergoing artillery drill still made Jackson the butt of their crude japes, pulling linch-pins from guns or caissons so that they would turn over, or otherwise prankishly sabotaging the routine. But they recognized and respected the metamorphosis: here was a seasoned warrior, training them in an art he had mastered under torrents of enemy fire. Crisp orders, clear purpose, bellowing voice—this was a very different man than the clumsy indoors professor.

THREE WOMEN

There was another side of Thomas Jackson, one that would have amazed his unsuspecting students and colleagues in the 1850's. During his Lexington years, three women helped the major blossom from a soldierly success and an academic mediocrity into a fully dimensional man. Jackson's relations with women had been significantly few and far between up to this point. He had never had much chance to know his mother, though in the fall of 1855 he traveled far to visit her unmarked grave and after the pilgrimage wrote of "her precious memory." Laura Jackson Arnold, Thomas's married sister, became for a time his favorite correspondent and confidante, though he did not see her much after their early years. Laura was impulsive and "rather temperamental," according to her neighbors in Beverly, Virginia. Her adult demeanor, so different from her brother's, puts the lie to modern notions that Tom Jackson's youthful years foreordained the rigid adult that he became. Laura never absorbed the religious tendencies that became central in Thomas's life, experienced sensational marital difficulties, and firmly rejected the Confederate cause. Federal soldiers occupying western Virginia would delight in visiting with the anti-Virginian sister of the South's most famous rebel.

The women who so dramatically affected Major Jackson during the 1850's were not related by birth but by marriage. Two wives and a sister-in-law became central features of Thomas's world. Elinor Junkin was the pleasant daughter of the Presbyterian-preacher president of Lexington's

Washington College. The even-tempered visage peering from her photograph seems to depict a plain woman. Major Jackson confirmed that objective judgment when he told a friend, "I used to think her plain, but her face now seems to me all sweetness." On August 4, 1853, Ellie and Tom were married. The newlyweds moved in with the Junkin family in the president's quarters.

Ellie Jackson's religious nature prodded Thomas toward the deeper spiritual commitment for which his soul was so well suited. Her devotion and tenderness—for the two were obviously deeply in love—opened emotional vistas the major had never experienced and hardly could have imagined. Their love story had a pathetically short run, however, because Mrs. Jackson died in childbirth on October 22, 1854, together with their son. Instead of completing a family, Thomas Jackson again had none. Three months later the distraught widower wrote to an uncle, "But what is life...I welcome its close." Five months after the disaster he told a West Point classmate that all he looked forward to from life was the event "which will emancipate me from this body...knowing that it is not far distant."

Margaret Junkin (later M. J. Preston) played the central role in pulling Major Jackson back from the abyss of depression. Maggie, who sorrowed for her sister every bit as much as Tom did for his wife, happened to be one of the brightest, most literate women in the South. The two eventually may have been attracted romantically, but Presbyterian canon (by then a polestar for Jackson) forbad such connection between former in-laws. With help from the brilliant Maggie, Thomas Jackson found solace and adjusted to his loss. At the same time he became familiar under her tutelage with a new world, that of the intellect. The library that Jackson amassed and used well—his signatures, annotations, and markings make that evident—included several languages and an encyclopaedic array of subjects. There was physics on the shelf for his job, and religion for his soul; but far more of history and biography, together with some philosophy and literature, including two excerpted collections of Shakespeare. The dull but determined Jackson of popular historical myth must dissolve on contact with evidence of the man's library and of his status as soulmate to the dazzling Margaret Junkin Preston.

In the summer of 1857, Jackson married Mary Anna Morrison, another daughter of a Presbyterian cleric and college president. Ten months later she bore a daughter, but the baby died within a few weeks. Thomas and Anna nonetheless carved out a bit of connubial bliss that constituted the longest stretch of intimate family life Jackson ever knew. The clumsy scientist and rigid soldier known to a tolerant, though unimpressed, pub-

Major Jackson in 1857.

lic became in private the tenderest of husbands. It was, a contemporary wrote, "something beautiful to see." In time, Jackson also embraced the Presbyterian faith with unswerving ardor. He had been baptized in that creed as an infant, and then as an Episcopalian in 1849. During the 1850s, the Lexington presbytery ordained what its preacher recognized as the best deacon he would ever find, driven by a "simple, earnest scriptural faith in God which dominated his whole being." An absolute, unreserved, fundamental religious ardor became the single most notable aspect of Thomas Jackson's private nature for the remainder of his life.

A combination of that unflinching piety with methodical deportment, rampant hypochondria, and an unpolished demeanor contributed to an aura of peculiarity that clings to the brow of Jackson's historical persona. Americans insist on at least a tincture of eccentricity in their heroes. A preacher with whom Jackson boarded for several months, however, derided such excesses of popular lore. "He was just a simple *gentleman,*" the clerical host insisted, "such as we meet in large numbers every day upon our streets...without ever once thinking whether there is anything singular about them or not."

As America careened toward civil war, Professor Jackson commanded the VMI artillery detachment sent to help police the hanging of John Brown. In the hotel where the Lexington men bivouacked, the major admonished one of them to hide his valuables in his socks. No thief would think to look there, and he could not forget them on dressing to leave. Jackson then put on clean socks in the morning and left his watch and wallet behind, to the intense delight of his rowdy young charges.

Major Jackson remained content in Lexington until the outbreak of war. He had found there a niche so comfortable and rewarding that no other life could seem more attractive. A brother-in-law, D. H. Hill, solicited his assistance in the design of a new military academy in North Carolina, to be modeled after VMI. Had Jackson relocated to that fledgling institution in the Old North State, his subsequent career clearly would have been different in unknowable—but significant—ways. As the ranking VMI faculty member with substantial military experience, the major grew in stature when war loomed. He played a crucial role in defusing a premature revolt among secessionist cadets, declaring in a brief address: "The time for war has not yet come, but...when it does come my advice is to draw the sword and throw away the scabbard." Not long thereafter Jackson led the corps of cadets out of Lexington, four days after Virginia seceded.

"LIKE A STONE WALL"

Major Jackson became Major General Jackson just five and one-half months after leaving Lexington. Being catapulted through a promotional spiral that added nearly one rank per month did not unman Jackson in the least. He had found the perfect stage upon which to perform. Thomas Jackson simply was cut out to be a warrior.

The road from VMI to everlasting fame took Jackson and his cadets to Richmond on April 22, 1861. Three days later Virginia's governor, striving frantically to defend the state without any military establishment in place, appointed Jackson to the rank of major of engineers. On the 27th a new and better commission arrived: colonel of Virginia volunteers. Two more days and Colonel Jackson reached the crucial frontier town of Harpers Ferry and assumed command. It was, he wrote his wife, "the post I prefer above all others." The colonel found an amusing array of unmilitary militia generals and an alarming mass of untrained, undisciplined soldiery. The generals departed in a huff when they found that the governor's orders superseded them; the men gradually succumbed to the drilling and discipline that Colonel Jackson imposed at a furious pace.

To accomplish the daunting task of defending Harpers Ferry with raw levies, Jackson assembled a staff of bright, competent young men. Many of them remained with him to the end of his life. The staff skilfully arranged a series of logistical endeavors: removing the invaluable ordnance equipment from the old U. S. arsenal; capturing railroad rolling stock and securing it for Confederate use; and arming and feeding the small army assembling under Jackson's direction. The results were striking. A captain from Culpeper wrote home: "I wish that Col. Jackson could have been [here] from the first. Those others were not Military Men." After four frenzied weeks of independent command, Jackson's role shifted when General Joseph E. Johnston arrived to take charge.

As fate would have it, Joe Johnston was as unlike Jackson as any one man could be: courtly, querulous, egocentric, terminally timid—and now, suddenly, Jackson's superior. Johnston at once began talking of abandoning Harpers Ferry, and in less than three weeks did so. On July 2, Jackson won a lively skirmish (it seemed at the time like a veritable Armageddon) above Harpers Ferry at Falling Waters, abetted substantially by some dashing cavalry under Colonel J. E. B. Stuart. By this time, though he did not yet learn of it for several days, Jackson had been promoted to brigadier general. General R. E. Lee sent the commission from Richmond on July 3; it took rank from June 17.

Jackson's command was made up of five infantry regiments of sturdy Shenandoah Valley men: the 2nd, 4th, 5th, 27th, and 33rd Virginia. The brigade headed on July 18 for a fateful date with destiny. When the hurried advance reached Paris, just east of Ashby's Gap, the general stood guard in person while his weary men slept. Federals marching southwest from Washington threatened the Confederate army around Manassas Junction. The Valley troops hurried eastward across the Blue Ridge, then mounted trains to continue toward the threatened point. Jackson reached Manassas late on July 19. Two days later the war's first major battle erupted along the banks of Bull Run. Federals turned the Confederate left flank and forced back the green, but deadly determined, Southern defenders. At the battle's climax, General Jackson held his regiments under firm control ("All is well," the men heard him say) behind the crest of the crucial Henry House Hill and provided a core on which the army rallied. "If you see any Yankees coming," he told his troops, "give them—pepper!" General Barnard E. Bee of South Carolina, struggling to control his own troops in the maelstrom, saw Jackson's stand and said something like: "There stands Jackson like a Stone Wall! Rally behind the Virginians." When the day was won, Jackson's role generally was recognized as central, even pivotal. America's most famous military nickname was born.

In the late-20th-century age of the anti-hero, it has become popular to dwell lovingly on a chatty late-life memoir that claimed, with knowledge received at third hand, that Bee really was *complaining* about Jackson standing still (like a stone wall) instead of coming forward to help him. The quibble is inane for a number of reasons, not least among them that it would have been monumentally foolish for Jackson to march in the direction that Bee is alleged to have wanted. Five more regiments of bewildered rookies would have accomplished nothing in the melee; as a stonewall-like rallying point, they turned the tide. Contemporary rumor suggested that Bee—known as "Bubble" to his mates in the Old Army—might have been intoxicated, albeit brave, on July 21. The merits of the case can effect only the most superficial of ironies, since the Richmond newspapers picked up the nickname for Jackson within days. The gleeful assignment by modern skeptics of most Confederate military merit to the crafty machinations of postwar "Lost Cause" manipulators can hardly gain much credence under that circumstance. One weary Southern infantryman filed a more legitimate complaint about the name. Forlornly examining his worn-out shoes, the dusty soldier declared "Stonewall" to be "a damned misnomer....He's a lion on the jump for prey."

THE LONE SENTRY.

Jackson's nickname promptly became a key element in what soon would be his legendary status. "Stonewall" resonates unlike most other historical sobriquets. Furthermore, it blended perfectly with its subject's personality and character, subtly making the man and the legend a comfortable fit in the popular mind. Without detracting in any way from Jackson's dazzling achievements, it is easy to imagine a less dramatic public profile today for just plain old General Thomas J. Jackson. Similarly, "Hero of the Valley" Jackson or "Old Reliable" Jackson probably would not carry the mysterious, deadly, yet somehow attractive aura that clings to "Stonewall" Jackson in the consciousness of those only casually aware of the facts. Jackson's new name also became an integral part of his country's language. Had he not conducted himself as he did on July 21, 1861, 20th-century political charlatans caught in their misdeeds almost certainly would not call their response "stonewalling," but rather "standing firm" or "clamming up," or "retreating into the bunker."

STONEWALL'S VALLEY

Modern Americans could survive without "stonewall" as part of the English lexicon, and they certainly could do very nicely without the political chicanery known as "stonewalling." The Confederate nation, however, quite likely would not have survived the summer of 1862 without the original "Stonewall" Jackson. After the battle of Manassas, the war in Virginia degenerated into eight months of stolid inaction. Measles and other diseases ravaged camps of rustics who never had been around so many germs, and who knew nothing of sanitation. Otherwise, all was indeed quiet along the Potomac every night. On October 7 Jackson was commissioned major general and a month later orders sent him to take over the protection of his beloved Valley of Virginia. The result was a campaign that remains one of the most famous in all of American military history. Before he could launch that campaign, however, Major General Jackson faced a daunting array of challenges from friend and foe alike.

Fortunately the general's reliable old Stonewall Brigade joined him in the Valley in November 1861. Around that nucleus Jackson doggedly built up near Winchester a little army with which to attempt great things. The militia companies Jackson called out proved to be of marginal value at best. Early in December three brigades of regular reinforcements arrived. They proved to be a mixed blessing, however, because of contentious and inadequate leaders. General William W. Loring simply did not suit Jackson's alert, aggressive command style. The commander of the first of Loring's brigades to arrive, William B. Taliaferro, never did find a way to

Library of Congress

Photo of Jackson taken in 1862.

get along with Jackson (although after Stonewall's death, Taliaferro sought to bask a bit in the dead hero's afterglow).

For a time Jackson's little command was styled the "Army of the Monongahela"; the overly optimistic cognomen—whether chosen by Jackson or assigned by a sanguine journalist—disappeared almost at once. It was in that westward direction, though, that the general made his opening move. On the first day of 1862, Jackson led his polyglot force out into the western mountains: the dependable Stonewall Brigade; Loring's large but ill-led force; and the raw militiamen. Balmy weather promptly turned cold, then bitterly cold, then even worse. Jackson prodded weary and freezing men over ice-clad roads north to the Potomac. A disgruntled colonel who saw the general helping lift a wagon out of a muddy hole muttered: "that is the business he ought always to be at." After he drove some Federals across the river, the determined Jackson turned west toward the mountain village of Romney. On January 14 the head of the column reached its goal. The army suffered almost no battle casualties, but it had undergone what a seasoned veteran would call "the most terrible experience" during four years of war.

Jackson was pleased with his success and envisioned expanding his strategic base even further. Loring and his officers forestalled that by complaining directly to Richmond about their distasteful situation. Jackson was using them too hard; surely anyone could see that this cold and desolate marching was not the way to fight a war. The malcontents suggested wintering "much more comfortably, and at much less expense" somewhere else.

A major crisis in Jackson's career, and in the history of the Confederacy, ensued. Judah P. Benjamin, Jefferson Davis's grotesque choice for Secretary of War despite a plenary lack of military experience or aptitude, agreed that Romney was not on *his* list of trophies to be sought. Davis, eager to meddle everywhere and always, joined Benjamin in ordering from afar that Jackson move all of his troops back to Winchester—without consulting either Jackson or his superior Joe Johnston. The two bureaucrats somehow contrived to know that a hostile column was about to cut off Romney (no such enemy existed). Jackson immediately resigned. "With such interference in my command, I cannot expect to be of much service...."

Stunned Virginians protested the loss. The Winchester newspaper damned "croakers and fault-finders." The governor and Jackson's favorite Congressman both appealed to their countryman's well-honed sense of duty and finally induced the general to remain with his command. One relieved soldier wrote: "everyone is rejoicing over it; he is beloved by all." Davis typically never recanted: the phantom column closing on Romney (which existed only in the president's fevered imagination) had required "prompt action," he insisted weeks later. Jackson henceforth recognized Davis as a deadly enemy in spirit and always studiously avoided him. Loring disappeared into relative oblivion. Some of his troops went too, but the best of them remained with Stonewall, who steadily molded them into an army. He soon would need their disciplined might. Melding them into his command took a good bit of Jackson's energy that winter. Among the devices he used to ensure order was an effort to destroy all distilleries in the region. Ever the pragmatist, the general earmarked the copper retrieved from these recreational apparatuses for delivery to Confederate ordnance shops. Stills, like ploughshares, might be turned into swords—or at least into cannon and percussion caps.

By the middle of March 1862, the basic circumstances of Jackson's famous Shenandoah Valley Campaign were taking form. Joe Johnston's Confederates had abandoned Manassas. Soon Federals under George B. McClellan would threaten Richmond from the southeast by means of a masterfully conceived water-borne invasion of the Peninsula. Because it ran from southwest to northeast, with its mouth north of Washington, the Valley lurked behind General McClellan as an apparent threat to the Federal capital. President Abraham Lincoln kept a weather eye on anything that might impinge upon his political bastion. Union forces obliged to keep Jackson from erupting out of the Valley would have been highly useful in McClellan's siege of Richmond, could they have gotten free to move in that direction. Jackson's strategic imperative, therefore, was to anchor his foe in the Valley. If he could destroy the Valley Federals, Jackson might then be able to go help lift the siege of the Confederacy's capital.

The necessity of keeping his enemy from leaving the Valley drove Stonewall to fight the Battle of Kernstown on March 23. He had been forced to abandon Winchester on March 11. Ten days later the army's cavalry chief, Turner Ashby, brought word that the Yankees were moving east out of the Valley; only a few regiments remained around Winchester, he thought. Ashby soon would become a major headache for Jackson because of his complete lack of organizational aptitude. But the cavalryman was unbelievably brave and dashing and a most reliable reconnaissance officer. This once, however, his information was flawed. When Jackson lashed his hard-marching column of 3,500 men to the southern edge of Winchester on the 23rd, he found nearly three times that many Yankees awaiting him.

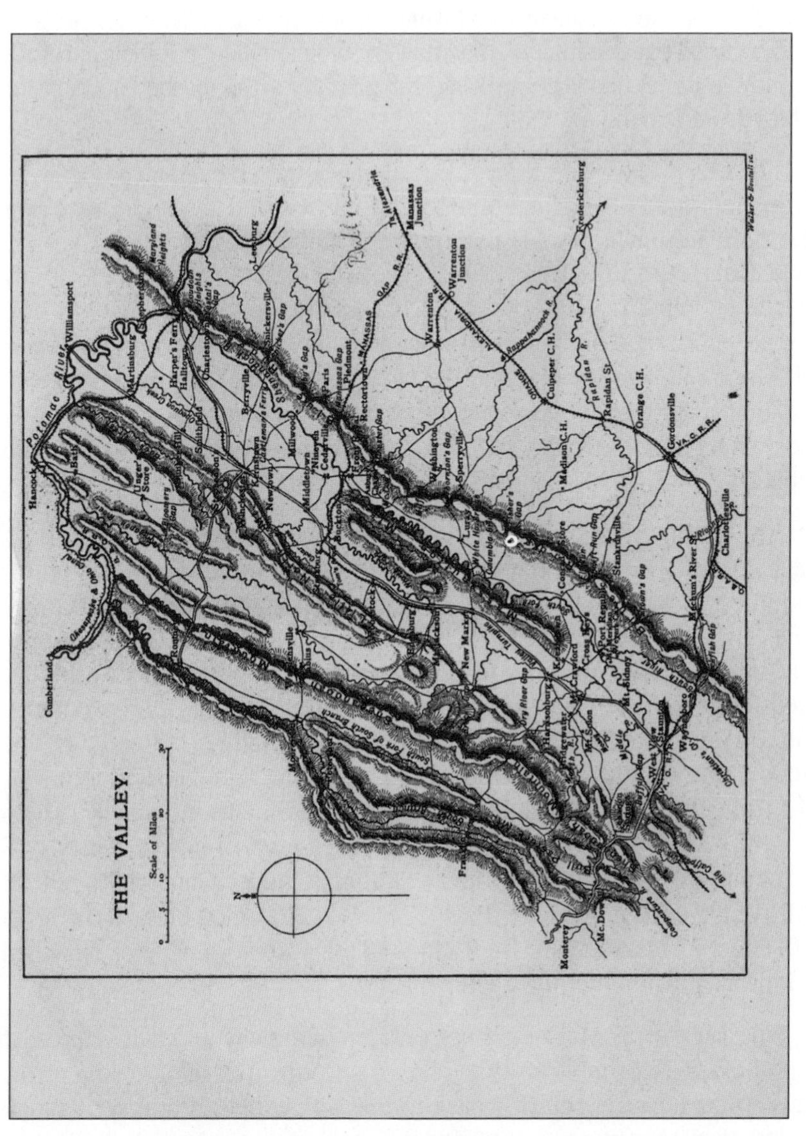

George F.H. Henderson, Stonewall Jackson and the American Civil War. *(London, New York: Longmans, Green & Co., 1898), opposite 214.*

Kernstown turned into a tactical nightmare. Confederate artillery based on the Valley Turnpike came under increasingly heavy fire. Infantry flung west of the pike to outflank the enemy foundered in the face of strong Federal reserves. The battle raged over a crucially situated stone wall. Jackson's regiments managed to disengage and retreat under cover of darkness, battered but still intact. They had not won the field, but their general's aggressive thrust had accomplished his primary mission: he had kept the enemy from leaving the Valley.

For nearly six weeks after Kernstown, Jackson played a careful waiting game. He fell back for a time to a strong position behind Stony Creek near Edinburg, then farther south and east to the unassailable fastness of Swift Run Gap in the Blue Ridge. There he lurked on the flank of any Federal attempt to march southward, across his front, toward the key railroad town of Staunton. Through what must have seemed an endless interval, Stonewall was forced to throttle back his aggressive instincts and wait impatiently for an opportunity to strike his foe. There were just too many Federals loose in the Valley for even the audacious Jackson to assault with impunity.

The advent of conscription that spring gave Jackson a chance to augment his army by enforcing the draft. To accomplish something significant, though, he needed a sizable infusion of strength. Some of that came from east of the mountains in the form of General Richard S. Ewell's troops. Jackson gathered the rest by forceful action. Leaving Ewell's freshly arrived force at Swift Run Gap, Stonewall marched his own division eastward on muddy roads, apparently away from the Valley. Beyond the Blue Ridge, however, the men boarded trains and came right back into the Valley. Unloading at Staunton, they pounded west into the mountains to help a friendly force under General Edward "Allegheny" Johnson. On May 8 the combined Confederates fought Unionists under General Robert H. Milroy above the mountain village of McDowell. "God blessed our arms with victory," Jackson wired to Richmond the next morning, then launched a vigorous pursuit after the fleeing enemy.

The success at McDowell not only chased away an enemy force; it also allowed Jackson to absorb Johnson's troops into his growing army. Thus strengthened he hurried back to the Valley, picked up Ewell's men around New Market and Luray, and then roared north through the Valley. An army that had been 3,500 strong at Kernstown now numbered more than 15,000 as it bore down on Front Royal on May 23, 1862. Only 1,000 men faced Jackson there, forlornly; the rest of Nathaniel P. Banks's Northern army remained impotent a dozen miles to the west in Strasburg.

After destroying the Front Royal detachment, Jackson should have been able to win easily a race against Banks to reach Winchester. But Jackson's strategic imperative imposed caution: he still must not let his enemies leave the Valley. Given his head start, Banks reached Winchester first. It did him little good. On May 25, Jackson launched a sweeping attack that drove the Yankees out of town and sent them scrambling toward the Potomac in a frantic rout. A rowdy Louisiana brigade led by General Richard Taylor led the attack. Residents of Winchester, relieved from a long spell of enemy occupation, raced deliriously through the streets with their victorious soldiers, shouting encouragement. Stonewall thanked God, as was his wont, and then looked for further opportunities.

Pushing all the way to the river, threatening Washington, would accomplish even more than thrashing Banks had done. Federal reaction threatened to cut Jackson's extended columns off at the end of May and the beginning of June. Jackson was unfazed. An aide came upon him lying against a tree a few feet behind a battery that was thundering steadily, "slumbering as placidly as an infant in its mother's arms." The hard marching that had turned the Valley infantry into "Foot Cavalry" ensured the army's safety. Most of it slipped through a tightening Yankee noose on June 1 and marched south. Rain falling in torrents made the Southerners miserable; it also aided them immensely by slowing pursuit across impassable rivers. Northerners chasing Jackson split into two columns, separated by the towering, fifty-mile-long Massanutten Mountain. At the southern tip of that massif, near Harrisonburg, Jackson slid southeastward to Port Republic, a hamlet at the head of the South Fork of the Shenandoah River.

The stage was set for the final, crowning achievement of Jackson's Valley Campaign. Massanutten kept the pursuing columns from getting together, and the river further complicated the Yankees' task. After nearly falling captive to an enemy raiding party early on June 8, Jackson fought two battles in two days and won them both. Ewell managed the Battle of Cross Keys on the 8th, four miles behind Port Republic; Jackson only rode to the vicinity once during the day. Federals under John C. Fremont failed to make any headway against Ewell's sturdy defense. The next morning Jackson launched his troops downstream from "Port" and waged a bitter struggle on the rich alluvial plain of the Lewis family farm. A seventy-foot-high knoll called "the Coaling" dominated the field. Confederate reinforcements were much delayed by a bottleneck at an ersatz bridge. Jackson impetuously threw the first troops to arrive against the formidable Union position—in vain. The action hung in the balance as Yankee infantry gradually gained the upper hand. Once again Taylor's Louisianians answered Jackson's call, taking the Coaling in a bitter hand-to-hand melee and ensuring victory.

With both Federal detachments soundly beaten and retiring precipitiously northward, Jackson stood triumphant in the Valley on June 10. During a ten-week campaign he had paralyzed 40,000 Federals while never employing many more than 15,000 soldiers. He had inflicted many more casualties then he had suffered. Far more importantly, he had held Federal attention on the Valley; had protected the Valley as his country's commissary storehouse; and had given Southerners hope at a time when no good news of any sort had been in evidence. A Georgia newspaper that had once wondered about Jackson's sanity now crowed: "It gives us a vertigo of delight to think of what Jackson has done. We hope he will keep on and give us an apoplexy before he stops." Now the hero of the Valley could head east toward Richmond and lend a hand in raising the siege of the capital of his state and his country. Beyond the Blue Ridge Jackson would find dramatic opportunities. But the Valley Campaign also had exacted a heavy toll on its victor. The exhausted general was headed for a week fraught with unaccustomed uncertainty and lassitude.

BEWILDERMENT AROUND RICHMOND

No one had heard of stress fatigue in 1862. Had such a diagnosis been current, admitting to the disorder would have been impossible for a man like Jackson in any event. Without knowing of the malady, Stonewall had it badly. All his life, Jackson required a good night's sleep to function optimally. The Valley Campaign had not offered much opportunity for rest. At its end, one of the staff wrote, "Gen. Jackson is completely broken down." The Confederates enjoyed a week of overdue rest after the triumphs at Cross Keys and Port Republic, but their general stayed diligently at work reorganizing and preparing the army for its next venture.

On June 18 Jackson started his Valley Army eastward, up the Blue Ridge and then down the other side. In the inevitable tangle of troops and trains that day, one of the staff gave voice to concern about arrangements for the night. Jackson turned to his aide and with customary earnestness delivered an epigram that strikingly illuminates his personal and professional mindset: "Never take counsel of your fears."

Intricate marching arrangements and complex tactical maneuvers that Jackson faced during the next fortnight proved to be beyond his ability to handle, not because he became fearful, nor because he was out of his depth: instead, he simply was worn to a frazzle. Getting to the vicinity of Richmond had cost Jackson enough effort and enough sleep to complete the debilitation that had left him "broken down" earlier in the month. All night on June 22-23 the general rode, covering more than 50 miles in 14 hours, to attend a meeting with R. E. Lee and his subordinate officers. He arrived "dusty, travel-worn, and apparently very tired," an eyewitness and friend wrote. After the conference, Jackson turned around and rode back, evidently without any sleep whatsoever on either night. The next afternoon he sat down and—incredibly, atypically—read a novel briefly, then took a listless nap. The officer who had come to personify energy and determination (and would do so repeatedly in the future) was becoming bewildered and disoriented.

Lee's army defending Richmond had been pressed back upon the capital city by a mammoth, if sluggish, Union force commanded by General George B. McClellan. The Chickahominy River, flowing across an arc northeast of the city, bisected McClellan's force. Lee hoped to bring Jackson's reinforcements in upon the enemy's exposed right flank and unravel the attackers' line. To combine converging columns in the face of an enemy is among the most difficult of all military accomplishments, even for a veteran army accustomed to fighting together. It did not work at all well in June 1862 for Confederates unfamiliar with one another. The story of the week of battles that lifted the siege of Richmond is one of columns that did *not* converge, day after day. In several instances the commander at fault was Jackson.

Lee's plan called for Jackson to arrive on June 26 close enough to the enemy right near Mechanicsville to force McClellan to recoil. Stonewall's troops, delayed by felled trees across the road and by enemy skirmishers, came on the scene too late to accomplish any good that evening. By the next morning the enemy had recognized the threat and pulled back eastward into a strong position behind Boatswain's Swamp near Gaines's Mill. Again Jackson's troops were to serve as the maneuver element, pushing beyond the Federal right. Again his column moved without the celerity and determination that had won the Valley ("slowly and awkwardly," an aide admitted); its head even wandered aimlessly off course for a time. An aide sent to Jackson on this day described the general's attire as including an "old sun yellowed tilt forward cap [and] dingy coat." When his troops finally reached the proper sector, Jackson rode into a hurricane of artillery fire to reconnoiter, then sat behind his line sucking on a lemon. A last mighty, desperate onslaught near dusk won the day on June 27. The

Jackson during the Seven Days, by a 19th century artist.

Army of Northern Virginia had won its first great battle. The enemy was far from destroyed, however, and Southern losses had been high.

During the two days of desultory action that followed Gaines's Mill, Jackson did no fighting, but succeeded in getting across the Chickahominy. Events on June 30 seemed to daze the normally resourceful Stonewall. He allowed the murky, sluggish waters of White Oak Swamp to stymie his entire force. Meanwhile, the rest of Lee's Confederates strove valiantly to damage McClellan's Federals at Frayser's Farm, just across the swamp from Jackson. An officer who saw the general that morning said that he "appeared worn down to the lowest point of flesh consistent with effective service. His hair, skin, eyes, and clothes were all one neutral dust tint." During the afternoon the weary Jackson slept while guns roared not far away. A cavalry officer reported finding what looked like a workable passage through White Oak Swamp; the general listened, said nothing, and soon fell asleep. An aide sent to headquarters to find out about the delay reported, "it looked to me as if...we were waiting for Jackson to wake up." Even when his eyes were open, Stonewall remained figuratively asleep all day long while his friends not far away fought desperately. Federal General William B. Franklin nicely summarized what everyone was thinking: "It is likely that we should have been defeated...had General Jackson done what his great reputation seems to make it imperative that he should have done."

Southern valor at Frayser's Farm on June 30 kept the enemy retreating, but Jackson's lethargy prevented Lee from winning the decisive victory he had envisioned. A Georgian who visited army headquarters saw a body sprawled beneath a table: "That is Stonewall," he was told; "he has had no sleep for forty-eight hours and fell down there exhausted." The campaign ended on July 1 with the bloody, futile battle of Malvern Hill, in which Jackson played a subordinate role. McClellan's siege of Richmond had been lifted in a series of battles that came to be called "the Seven Days Campaign," but his army had not been destroyed. Confederates of all ranks wondered what had become of the energetic victor of the Valley. Jackson had operated independently there; Lee now worried that Jackson might not work well in tandem. Some thought he was jealously preserving his own troops at the expense of others. One day of delay had been Sunday: might the devout Stonewall have refused to move on that basis (ignoring his record of Sabbath battles in the Valley)? Theorists offered a wide array of reasons for the disappointing showing. Jackson never responded. The best indication that the general recognized that he was not himself came on the evening of June 30 at the end of his worst day of the war, with all of its missed opportunities at White Oak Swamp. After Jackson dozed at dinner with a biscuit in his mouth, he bestirred himself and said to his staff: "Now, gentlemen, let us at once to bed, and rise with the dawn, and see if to-morrow we cannot *do something*!"

TO THE PLAINS OF MANASSAS AGAIN

One Confederate disappointed by Jackson's showing around Richmond aptly summarized the aftermath from the perspective of mid-1863: "as if to make up for it, he had ever since been almost two Jacksons." The lethargy of June 1862 never reappeared, even momentarily, as Stonewall carved out a legend built on rapid marches, brisk attacks, and an unblemished array of successes.

Just two weeks after the end of the Seven Days campaign around Richmond, Lee sent Jackson north to confront a new Federal army commanded by General John Pope. Before marching away on his new assignment, Jackson, characteristically, scribbled a check for $150 to the Bible Society of the Confederate States of America. On July 27, Lee ordered A. P. Hill's large division to move to Jackson's support. The commanding general also forwarded some avuncular advice to his taciturn subordinate, suggesting the prudence of taking Hill into his confidence as a means of effective management.

Jackson completely ignored Lee's advice, and as a consequence he and Hill were at loggerheads almost at once. Despite that deadly antipathy, the two Confederate leaders crafted a hard-fought victory over Pope's advance guard at Cedar Mountain on August 9. The meeting engagement in the rolling countryside south of Culpeper Court House hung in the balance for a time as a Federal attack unraveled much of Jackson's ill-formed line. At the crisis, Stonewall rode into the melee, trading on his name and fame to rally his soldiers, a battle flag in one hand and his sheathed sword in the other, with enemy infantry on three sides. This closest sustained hostile personal encounter of the war must have been what prompted Jackson to call Cedar Mountain, in his wife's words, "the most successful of his exploits." The tactical confusion of that day hardly warranted such enthusiasm. The timely arrival of several of A. P. Hill's seasoned brigades gave Jackson a preponderance of force adequate to sweep the field. As darkness fell, the Confederates emerged triumphant. Jackson had inflicted twice as many casualties as he had suffered. After standing for two days on the ground he had won, Jackson moved back across the Rapidan River to await the arrival of Lee and the rest of the Army of Northern Virginia.

Cedar Mountain proved to be the last battlefield that Jackson commanded independently. In the ninth months of life left to him, Stonewall would become an incomparable executive officer to Lee as the two men forged the Army of Northern Virginia into the apparently invincible bulwark of the Confederate nation. They began by "suppressing" John Pope, as Lee termed the defeat of the boastful Northerner known for his draconian policy toward Southern civilians. Lee moved the rest of his army north to join Jackson, arriving in person on August 15. An attempt to trap Pope between the Rapidan and Rappahannock rivers foundered on some confusion within the ranks of the Southern cavalry.

With Pope safely behind the Rappahannock, Jackson moved leftward and upstream, hoping to get beyond the enemy right. On August 24 he and Lee agreed on an initiative that launched one of the epic marches in American military annals. Rather than side-slipping any farther, Jackson would cut entirely loose from the army and swing wide to the west while looping all the way around Pope and into his rear. On the 25th and 26th Jackson's column covered more than fifty miles, leaving Lee and the other half of the army to face the far larger, but mystified, Federal army across the Rappahannock. The stunning daring of the attempt was its primary protection. Rapid marching was—as so often with Stonewall's initiatives—the other key to success. A soldier heard the general earnestly reminding a brigade commander during this campaign, "Very few commanders properly appreciate the value of celerity." When Jackson's men captured key railroad depots far to Pope's rear, they revelled in confiscated food and luxuries long unavailable in the South. Their presence so far behind the Federal army sent shockwaves in every direction.

As Northern units recoiled frantically toward what had been their rear to cope with the startling threat, Lee and the rest of his troops moved along Jackson's route to join the raiders. Stonewall found a strong defensive position along an unfinished railroad grade in which to await the arrival of friends. Late on August 28, when a Federal column marched across his front, Jackson flung his men forward into the enemy's flank. They attacked with "a hoarse roar like that from cages of wild beasts at the scent of blood," an eyewitness reported. The bloody, drawn fight that ensued riveted Pope's attention and opened the Second Battle of Manassas, much of it fought on the same ground as the battle of July 1861 in which Stonewall won his *nom de guerre*.

For much of August 29, Jackson's men stood alone in the cuts and fills of the railroad bed against a succession of attacks. Some of the Federal lunges broke through temporarily. A Georgian saw Jackson riding

Woodcut of Jackson from photo taken in 1862.

Robert U. Johnson and Clarence C. Buel, eds., *Battles and Leaders of the Civil War.* (New York: The Century Co., 1887-88), Vol. 1, 121.

behind the line, exhorting the men and "praying aloud." When the enemy attack drew close enough for musketry, the general "ceased praying and commenced shouting...and urging on the boys." To a hard-pressed division commander, Jackson rasped curtly: "I'll expect you to beat them!" When ammunition ran low in an embattled South Carolina brigade, Stonewall rasped, "We will give them the bayonet." That afternoon Lee and General James Longstreet and the rest of the army began arriving to extend Jackson's right in a broad obtuse angle.

Pope did not recognize Lee's arrival on the 29th (thirty years later he was still denying that it had happened), but Jackson was mightily relieved. On the 30th, Pope attacked again toward the railroad, exposing his left to the fresh Confederate troops there. They attacked into the enemy flank and routed it, concluding one of the greatest Southern victories of the war. Jackson's initiative, daring, hard marching, and tenacious fighting had been the central feature of the triumphant campaign. His strikingly successful collaboration with Lee boded well for future operations. "I would follow him blindfolded," Jackson said of Lee at about this time, and meant it. The two leaders operated in harmony to a degree unparalleled elsewhere in the Southern armies. A staff officer reported that Stonewall "once said that the only objection he had to Genl Lee was that he did not hate Yankees enough."

INTO MARYLAND

While chasing Pope back into the defenses of Washington, Jackson won a short, intense battle in a rainy downpour at Ox Hill or Chantilly on September 1. With the Federals in disarray, Lee grasped the opportunity to raid into Maryland, crossing the Potomac on September 5. His old opponent, McClellan, kept the Army of the Potomac army between Lee and the capital city. From headquarters near Frederick on September 10, Jackson moved rapidly on another daring undertaking. Lee had determined to divide his army into five segments as part of an intricate plan. He intended to have Jackson push back south of the Potomac and quickly capture the Union garrison at Harpers Ferry, without giving McClellan a chance to overwhelm the rest of the army.

The plan worked, thanks to Jackson's determination and energy, although not so promptly as had been hoped. On September 15, he accepted the surrender of some 12,000 Yankees at Harpers Ferry. Massive piles of ordnance and other stores also fell into his hands. As the dusty and disheveled general galloped through the captured village, Federal prisoners pushed their guards ahead of them to the roadside to see the famous man. "The Yankees waved their caps too, and cheered him, just as we did," a South Carolinian wrote. "I wish we had him!" the captives muttered: "He's not much for looks, but if we'd had him we wouldn't have been caught in this trap." Another Yankee taken prisoner during this campaign told his captors, "of all men in this world, I would rather see Jackson." A Northern officer remarked enviously to his captors: "You can never whip soldiers who love their leaders as you do."

There was no time to savor the victory. Federal discovery of Lee's battle order gave McClellan the impetus to press westward across South Mountain's gaps. Jackson left A. P. Hill's division behind to parole the Harpers Ferry prisoners and process the other booty while he marched hard to rejoin the army near the village of Sharpsburg. The crisis developing there soon forced him to order Hill to march too, leaving only a token force at Harpers Ferry.

Near Sharpsburg, Lee was forming a line parallel to Antietam Creek and with the Potomac at his back. Jackson's half of the army held the Confederate left, where the first Northern onslaught fell early on September 17. Circumstances offered no opportunity for the aggressive initiatives that Stonewall favored. Instead he faced a deadly defensive struggle. In the bloody Cornfield, in front of the West Woods, and around the shell-torn Dunkard Church, Jackson shuffled his ranks and employed reserves as they arrived. The lines he knit together were barely able to hold their positions. As Jackson and General Lafayette McLaws held a hurried conference on horseback, a shell crashed into the group and wounded a courier, but spared the generals by not exploding. His ranks dreadfully thinned by straggling and losses, Jackson held on by virtue of the deadly tenacity so characteristic of his battlefield performance—and because of the unwavering bravery of the men he throw into the breach time and again. McClellan cooperated with the desperate Confederates by attacking piecemeal, from his right to his left.

By mid-day Jackson's tattered legions had passed the test. Weary and famished, the general happened upon his chief surgeon eating a peach, appropriated the doctor's entire supply, "and literally devoured them." Meanwhile, McClellan's uncertain efforts gravitated farther south, out of Stonewall's sector. For a time he contemplated an offensive on the left to relieve pressure on the rest of the line, but General Jeb Stuart brought word of overpowering enemy strength and it became obvious that simply persevering in a defensive posture and trusting to luck was the wisest course. Sunset ended the Confederate ordeal, but Lee refused to retreat. Only on the night of September 18-19 did the army recross the Potomac near Shepherdstown. When a sizable enemy force incautiously splashed across in pursuit, abetted by the arrant ineptitude of Confederate artillery General William Nelson Pendleton, Jackson turned his infantry and briskly flung the Northerners back into the river with heavy loss.

FREDERICKSBURG

The lovely Shenandoah Valley offered the ideal arena for reorganizing and reinvigorating an army exhausted and battered by a summer of intense campaigning. In that fertile country, men and horses found food and rest. Confederate quartermasters gradually coped with the challenge of supply, although thousands of soldiers were still shoeless as wintry weather approached. The organization of the army itself underwent a metamorphosis during that fall of 1862. Lee had long used Jackson as a corps commander, but Confederate law made no provision for corps, nor for lieutenant generals to command them. When the Congress finally rectified that oversight, Lee recommended Jackson heartily for the promotion. The army commander's note to Jefferson Davis, however, revealed obliquely some uncertainty that Lee had once—but no longer—felt about Jackson after the Seven Days fiasco. Lee's opinion of Stonewall "has been greatly enhanced," he told the president. "He is true, honest, and brave; has a single eye to the good of the service, and spares no exertion to accomplish his object." All of that enthusiastic endorsement hinted at earlier concerns: Lee clearly had had room for a "greatly enhanced" opinion, and now was delighted to be able to attest to traits not patently apparent at some point.

Jackson's view of Lee had never wavered. He had told a staff officer in 1861 that the United States Army's success in the Mexican War had been due in large part to Lee's exertions there. Stonewall had become what an observer called "the motive power that executes, with the rapidity of lightning, all that Lee can plan." The fabulous collaboration between the two officers had a few more months of success ahead. It remains one of the most famous and successful military combinations of all time.

Lieutenant General Jackson took rank from October 9, 1862. His corps remained in the Valley near Winchester when Lee and the rest of the army marched east across the Blue Ridge to oppose a new Union commander, General Ambrose E. Burnside. On November 25 Jackson rode through Fisher's Gap en route to join Lee in the vicinity of Fredericksburg. He would never again see his beloved Valley.

The Confederate position that Lee had chosen on high ground beyond Fredericksburg offered tremendous advantages to the defense. Lee could hardly believe that Burnside would assail him there, so he sent Jackson down the Rappahannock to forestall any enemy crossings in that direction. Early on December 11 Burnside launched his army over the river right at Fredericksburg. During the next two days Jackson's corps marched back and rejoined the main army. As Stonewall scouted on foot toward the enemy to examine their positions, a sharp-eyed Northerner fired a bullet that whistled shrilly between the general and his aide, James Power Smith. With unaccustomed drollery, Jackson murmured: "Mr. Smith, had you not better go to the rear? They may shoot you!" Soon the general's colleagues were poking gentle fun at him when he appeared along the Fredericksburg lines wearing a braid-bedizened new uniform in startling contrast to his customary disheveled outfit. "Stonewall has drawed his bounty and has bought himself some new clothes!" a soldier quipped.

Although they comprised one-half of Lee's infantry, Jackson's late arrivals finally occupied less than one-fourth of the main line. Their late arrival precluded reshuffling responsibilities across the entire seven-mile-long Confederate front. That extra depth came in handy in the early afternoon of December 13 when a brave Federal attack broke through Jackson's position. Perhaps less alert and focused when standing on the defensive, Stonewall left a stretch of more than 500 yards along his front undefended. Some swampy thickets in that sector seemed to make it poor ground for the Northerners to attack across: but of course the assailants veered away from blazing muskets elsewhere into this less deadly space and surged through the gap. The lapse was the more astonishing because Jackson had remarked, "The enemy will attack here." General Maxcy Gregg of South Carolina was mortally hit during the breakthrough. There were not enough of the enemy to effect a permanent lodgment, and the unaccustomed depth of Jackson's reserves ensured the eventual victory. Nonetheless, Jackson's careless alignment caused the only concern, even if momentary, to a Confederate army that won an easy and resounding victory at Fredericksburg.

After a screaming Confederate counterattack rippled across Jackson's front and then receded, having restored the line, the general characteristically began plotting a new aggressive move. As that prospect fomented in Jackson's mind, a staff officer wrote, "his countenance glowed as from the glare of a great conflagration." The notion proved to be more wishful than practical. A blaze of hostile artillery fire changed Jackson's mind before he was able to unleash his men. The general went to back to his headquarters that night and fell fast asleep while sitting bolt upright on a stool. Long before dawn the next morning he visited the nearby Yerby house, where Maxcy Gregg lay dying in agony. The corps commander dismissed Gregg's talk of a rift between them and urged the South Carolinian to "turn your thoughts to God and to the world to which you go." Soon thereafter when an aide ruminated about how to deal with the seemingly endless tide of Yankees swarming across Virginia, Jackson responded abruptly: "Kill them, sir! Kill every man!" In that unflinching mood he entered the last winter of his life.

PLAIN, DIFFICULT, AND TENDER

By the end of 1862, Jackson had become about the most famous man in the English-speaking world. Almost no one obliged to deal at close hand with the general, however, knew what to make of the enigmatic hero. He was the cynosure of all eyes, but most observers commented with disappointment about Stonewall's entirely unprepossessing appearance: "a very plain man"; "wholly devoid of grace...awkward and embarrassed"; "makes one think of an old fox hunter"; "looked..like a Jew pedlar"; "looks like an old Virginia farmer"; "has an embarrassed, diffident manner"; "what a common, ordinary looking man he is!"; "seems a plainly dressed captain of cavalry, with an unpretending staff"; "there's nothing at all striking in his appearance"; "prematurely old, his face rather sharp...lips thin and often blue."

A distinct air of determination emanated from Jackson's otherwise "common, ordinary" appearance. Observers professed to notice "goodness stamped on his countenance"; "his face shows energy and decision"; "expression of his face [reveals] self-command, perseverance, indomitable will"; "rather an abstracted air"; "he had the dignity of quiet & silence." One of the men who knew Jackson best confirmed the accuracy of those who observed strength in the general's silence: "His will kept [him] steady....Selected his topic of thought & kept his mind to it....duty was preeminent—patriotism a passion & his religion embraced, as supreme. His *will* unsurpassed—fearless, unwearied, unchanging—persistent & it worked marvelous. He enthroned duty as the sovereign & insisted upon obedience—absolute...he feared neither himself nor anything or body."

The general's most famous war horse, "Little Sorrel," was about as plain as his master. Jackson's friend, Congressman Alexander R. Boteler, described the animal as "obedient, patient, easy-going and reliable...more serviceable than showy, and, altogether, as sober-sided...as any Presbyterian elder, with plain tastes and a practical turn, need desire to have about him." A North Carolinian thought Jackson's mount "sorry looking"; another Tar Heel simply called Little Sorrel "ugly"; A Georgian described the animal as a "dark, raw, bony horse, in poor condition." Jackson sat astride the animal "stark and stiff in the saddle," "an excellent rider but...awkward & ungraceful." The general's other mounts were no better: he "never had a decent looking horse during the war," according to one of his staff.

Plain looks did not diminish the general's stature amongst his troops once he came to symbolize victory. "His men," one of them wrote, "almost worship him." Lee inspired loyalty, even awe, but an army correspondent admitted that "he does fail to excite the same enthusiasm as Jackson." A Georgian loved and admired Lee, "but in a different way"; shouts generated by Jackson's passing were "almost deafening," but "I never heard [Lee] cheered...." Another observer reported that the army thought highly of Lee—"but the idol of the army, as well as of the people, is the gallant Stonewall Jackson." A South Carolinian wrote to his wife that "the whole army was carried away with excitement" when Jackson passed. "I never was so struck with any man as with him on that occasion." Astonishingly, Northerners were almost as much smitten with this most famous Rebel. An English visitor observed in the fall of 1862, "In the Northern cities Stonewall Jackson is the national hero."

Officers obliged to report directly to the unbending corps commander were not nearly so adulatory. During the early stages of the Valley Campaign, most of Jackson's subordinates would have echoed General Ewell's lament: "Did you ever see such damn foolishness?" Ewell called his commander "that enthusiastic fanatic," and described to J. E. B. Stuart in May 1862—ten days before Jackson's victorious advance down the Valley—how Stonewall had made "great mistakes" and was foolishly focused on local matters at the expense of affairs east of the mountains. General Richard Taylor left the Valley to visit Richmond in an attempt to have Jackson relieved. (Taylor came back convinced that he had persuaded Jefferson Davis—his brother-in-law—to send Longstreet out to relieve Jackson, a ludicrous notion that of course never materialized.) Valley cavalry chieftain Turner Ashby told a member of Congress that he personally had "saved the army...from being utterly destroyed" by Jackson's incompetence for months in early 1862. Jackson wrote to the same Congressman that he must oppose Ashby's promotion because of the cavalryman's inattention to organization and discipline. General Charles S. Winder, commanding Jackson's old brigade, told his diary: "Jackson is insane"; "disgusted with

Communion in Stonewall Jackson's camp.

Jackson"; "requesting to leave his command." The first-hand view of Stonewall in the spring of 1862 obviously did not include much of the unreserved applause so familiar in later descriptions. Even those subordinates not actually at loggerheads with Jackson found him aloof. He addressed no one in the entire army by a given name except for his bright young staff officer "Sandie" Pendleton.

Victory piled upon victory changed much of the tone of subordinates' comments. Nothing, however, ever relieved the personal discomfort that most felt when dealing directly with the inflexible Jackson. Ashby and Winder died unhappy, but at their posts. Ewell and Taylor became, tardily, bemused admirers. In the army's most famous court martial, General Richard B. Garnett defended himself with some success against a bill of particulars that Stonewall levied against him over the Battle of Kernstown: all of the regimental officers involved in the proceedings sided with Garnett against Jackson.

An even more famous quarrel, which never reached formal proceedings, involved Jackson and A. P. Hill. In November 1861 Jackson had eagerly sought to have Hill put in command of his own Stonewall Brigade (he had wanted Robert E. Rodes if he couldn't get Hill for the job, but wound up with Garnett). The following August, however, Jackson and Hill became bitter adversaries during the march that led to the Battle of Cedar Mountain. Jackson behaved with his customary excessive secrecy, leaving Hill uncertain how to behave; for his part, Hill was less energetic about marching arrangements than he ought to have been. For months the two men snarled at each other in written notes and through their staffs. Hill called Jackson a "crazy old Presbyterian fool." Every prickly note between the two carried the seeds of a new eruption. During the early months of 1863, open warfare before a military court seemed inevitable. Lee's gentle attempts to promote a reconciliation for the good of the cause failed for months, but in April the two generals somehow effected a rapprochement.

Another role the general played with gusto during this last winter of his life was that of doting father. He had not yet seen baby Julia (who was named for his mother), even though she had been born on November 23 and the new father learned of the event within five days. Typically, he told no one in the army about the joyous news. Some staff members only heard of the birth indirectly a month later. At his winter headquarters in the yard of "Moss Neck," home of the Corbin family, Stonewall enjoyed the companionship of a surrogate daughter. Janie Corbin, five-and-a-half years old, vivacious and pretty, visited him daily and always found a special treat saved for her by the man who was the terror of his enemies—and of his subordinates. One day, lacking any other gift, Jackson cut the braid off his military cap and gave it to the youngster to put in her hair. Janie once dashed up to her friend the general in the yard "and clasping her arms around one of his legs cried 'Genl Jackson kiss me please.'" The assembled officers laughed and Jackson "blushed like a girl." On the day that corps headquarters moved away from Moss Neck, Janie died of scarlet fever. When he heard the dreadful news, the mighty victor of many a bloody battlefield wept.

A few weeks later Jackson enjoyed one of the happiest moments of his life when he met a train at Guiney Station and saw his own baby girl for the first time—and his wife for the first time in more than a year. At the Yerby house, near Hamilton's Crossing on Fredericksburg battlefield, the general and his little family spent nine delightful days. Anna persuaded her husband to sit for a photographer on April 25. An attempt to induce General Lee to participate in the photo session failed, depriving posterity of a joint image of the Confederacy's two legendary leaders. During this family idyll, Jackson's favorite Presbyterian cleric baptized baby Julia. "Isn't she a little gem?" the proud father exclaimed. An aide watching the general parade Julia around on his shoulder mused, "What a wonderful future that little girl has!" Jackson responded, "I am not thinking of the future, I am only enjoying the present." The general's future that baptismal evening stretched ahead only seventeen days.

CONFEDERATE HIGH TIDE

A rainy spring delayed the onset of operations in 1863. On April 29, however, it became obvious that the Federal army opposite Fredericksburg was moving to the attack. Jackson left his wife and baby at the Yerby place and headed toward the sound of the guns. When it became obvious that Thomas would not return soon, Anna dashed off a note to "My precious husband." In phrases familiar to women who have sent their men off to war over the millennia she wrote feelingly: "I commend you, my precious darling, to the merciful keeping of the God of battles & do pray most earnestly for the success of our army this day. Oh! that our Heavenly Father may *preserve & guide & bless you* is my most earnest prayer....Our little darling will miss dearest Papa....God bless & keep you, my darling, Your devoted little wife."

Jackson and Lee watched enemy soldiers feint below Fredericksburg on the 29th, but soon recognized that a deadly threat hung over the Con-

Jackson just before Chancellorsville, sketch drawn by Lt. Frederick F. Fousse, 25th Virginia Infantry.

West Virginia and Regional History Collection, West Virginia University Libraries.

federate rear. General Joseph Hooker, the new commander of the Federal Army of the Potomac, had moved a strong column up the Rappahannock River with skill and daring and marshalled it several miles behind the Southern line around Fredericksburg. The absence of two divisions of infantry, which were off on a foraging mission in southeast Virginia, left Lee and Jackson with fewer than one-half as many men as their foe could muster. The missing men included corps commander James Longstreet. Free from Longstreet's fettering influence and attitude to dampen their military initiative, Lee and Jackson launched a dazzling series of marches and maneuvers. The results befuddled Hooker and led to the most astonishing Confederate victory of the war—and simultaneously to the Confederacy's most damaging loss.

Early on May 1 Jackson rode west at the head of his veteran infantry. On the high, open ground around Zoan Church on the Orange Turnpike he found a hard-pressed Confederate detachment and at once assumed command of the field. The careful defensive measures that the Southerners had been employing no longer mattered. Mighty Stonewall would attack, even though the country in front swarmed with far more enemy than he could match. Jackson's impact on the troops was, as always, electric. "Immediately we knew," wrote an artillery colonel, "we were going out on the warpath." The bright young gunner, not at all given to emotional hyperbole, enthused of Jackson: "as a fighter and a leader he was all that it can ever be given a man to be. How splendidly the pair of them [Jackson and Lee] looked to us, & how the happy confidence of the men in them shone in everyone's face...."

On the warpath was indeed where Jackson was bound. The overwhelming Federal might in front of him was diluted considerably by the dense thickets of the Wilderness of Spotsylvania. Only those troops maneuvering along the two roads (the Turnpike and the Orange Plank Road) bisecting the Wilderness could fight effectively. Jackson's indomitable will pushed his men forward along those two roads and nudged Hooker's troops back toward the country crossroads called Chancellorsville. A third corridor through the brushy tangle gave Stonewall another option. Using the grade of an unfinished railroad, he threw a brigade of Georgians past the enemy's exposed right flank and obliged it to curl back to the north.

As darkness quelled the fighting on May 1, Jackson had corralled the much larger Federal army around Chancellorsville, but its right extended westward uncontested for another three miles. At the uninhabited intersection of two country roads, the corps commander and the army com-

The last meeting of Lee and Jackson, May 1, 1863.

Johnson and Buel, eds., *Battles and Leaders of the Civil War*, Vol. 3, 204.

mander made a joint bivouac and considered their options for renewing the fight in the morning. They fully intended, as was their preference and custom, to retain the initiative—but how and where, in the face of Hooker's hordes?

Lee had reconnoitered in person on the right, toward the river, and found no opening worthy of serious consideration. Men from each general's staff crept forward through the moonlit woods to examine the prospects right in front, toward Chancellorsville. They brought back a negative report: the enemy was very strong there, and entrenching earnestly.

Retreat was unthinkable, both spiritually and pragmatically under the circumstances. What of a move leftward, against the Federal right? Word gradually arrived from the left of a dangerous but intriguing opportunity. A set of wagon roads twisting narrowly through the Wilderness led far enough west to get beyond Hooker's right, perhaps without being observed. By marching across the enemy's front (in contravention of one of the most basic rules for waging war), Jackson might be able to get clear behind the enemy force and damage it seriously with a surprise onset. Once the notion seemed practicable, Lee told Jackson to make the attempt. During the night further details arrived from cavalry scouts exploring the ground; from local civilians eager to be helpful; and from one of Jackson's Presbyterian-preacher friends, whose brother lived in that direction. Jackson scrawled a crude map in pencil to illustrate the project. At one point the generals spread broom straw on the surface of a box as they contemplated the undertaking; Jackson swept the straw off the surface in an animated gesture, no doubt showing how he intended to complete the mission.

Early on May 2 Jackson disappeared into the woods in execution of the most exciting and challenging orders he ever received. With nearly 30,000 men he was to make an hours-long march at great risk in order to get all the way around the Federals. As his men started on the daring venture, Jackson strode up to Lee's horse, leaned an arm on its neck, and talked "very earnestly and rapidly" to his chief, gesticulating energetically as he did so. The two Confederate warriors would never see each other again. After the war, in fact soon after the battle, questions arose about the genesis of the famous flank movement. Had it been Jackson's initiative, with Lee's concurrence? Or had Lee conceived the brilliant and daring attempt and then placed its execution, as he so often did, in the hands of his incomparable lieutenant? The planning was done in full collaboration, of course, but there is ample evidence that the idea originated with Lee. He said so in writing, with bluntness unaccustomed for so modest a man, on at least two occasions.

Jackson's desperately dangerous march must cover more than a dozen miles to reach the Federal rear, and do so without being discovered. Less than a mile into the route, open ground exposed the Confederate column to hostile eyes—and eventually enemy shells—from high ground in Federal hands well to the north. Unionist regiments sent south to investigate collided near Catharine Furnace with Southerners thrown out to protect Jackson's route. Some fierce small-scale fighting developed. The rear of the marching column had to detour away from the pressure point on an alternate set of woods roads. Through most of May 2 the men slogged wearily through the Wilderness. In accordance with a printed general order circulated to them nineteen days before, they marched two miles in fifty minutes, then rested for ten. Despite the measured pace, men fell out on the roadside panting and exhausted; this was their first strenuous effort after a winter on short rations. Early in the afternoon the flanking column reached the Orange Plank Road, where Jackson had thought he could turn east. Cavalry General Fitzhugh Lee showed Stonewall from a commanding knoll that Federals stretched west beyond the mouth of that road. Jackson scribbled a note to Lee—their last correspondence—about his change of plans: "The enemy has made a stand at [Melzi] Chancellor's, which is about two miles from Chancellorsville. I hope as soon as practicable to attack. I trust that an ever kind Providence will bless us with great success." He added a postscript about how well closed the column remained, then eagerly moved forward to plan his attack.

Soon after 5 p.m. Stonewall Jackson had arranged two full divisions and part of a third in lines perpendicular to the Orange Turnpike. They faced at right angles to the unsuspecting Federals before them, and overlapped the Unionists a mile on either side—having "crossed their T," a naval tactician would have called it. As the Southern infantrymen boiled out of the woods into the midst of their surprised enemies, screaming the Rebel Yell, they established the highwater mark of their famous army. For more than two miles Jackson and his men drove a full corps of Yankees, quickly surrounding and obliterating any brave knots of resistance. When the triumphant troops saw Stonewall riding nearby, they shouted their appreciation so loudly that the ground seemed "to tremble, as if shaken by an earthquake." The confusion inherent in a great victory inevitably disorganized and slowed the attackers, then darkness robbed the advance of the capacity to regroup. (Oh, for a few more hours of sun, such as Joshua had won for his army in Jackson's beloved Old Testament.)

A DEADLY SMOOTHBORE VOLLEY AND AN IRREPARABLE LOSS

Jackson rode forward at about 9 p.m. to look for a means to exploit the momentum he had created. If he could renew the attack, perhaps he might cut Hooker off from the river crossings several miles in his rear. Two staff officers and six couriers accompanied the general on his short, ill-fated ride. The little entourage did not venture more than 100 yards beyond the infantry line. It never reached the outermost friendly pickets. An unrelated brush between confused detachments in dark woods far south of Jackson triggered a spate of firing that spread steadily, almost instantaneously, across the front. Soldiers of the 18th North Carolina unleashed a volley from their antiquated smoothbore muskets that ought not to have posed much danger to Jackson. He was far enough forward to be near the extreme range for such weapons, and the tangled growth of the Wilderness shielded him from most of the Carolinian muzzles. Six members of the general's party escaped unscathed and seven of the nine horses were not hit. Nonetheless, three bullets hit Jackson. The God in whom Stonewall reposed such total confidence clearly had not intervened on his behalf at this deadly moment.

Despite having wounds in both arms, Jackson somehow controlled his panicky mount long enough for aides to take over and lead him toward the nearby main road. They tenderly lifted the general off "Little Sorrel" and placed him on the ground. General A. P. Hill, who had escaped the same volley unhit, hurried to Jackson's side and a knot of staffers gathered around. Someone quickly sent away for a surgeon and called for a tourniquet. Jackson had suffered two wounds that mangled his left arm, breaking bones so badly that they protruded through skin. Another ball went through his right palm. Branches had gouged disfiguring but relatively minor wounds across his face when his horse dashed away in terror.

The first surgeon who reached the stricken general discovered with some surprise that his patient was not bleeding badly. He rejected the tourniquet when it arrived, instead using only handkerchiefs to bind the wounds and make a sling. Then eager hands put the general on a stretcher and started him toward the rear. At that moment a torrent of artillery fire swept the road and forced the bearers to put the stretcher down and lie beside it. Three aides used their prone bodies to shield the general, watching in awe as canister rounds struck the road on all sides, sending up bright blue sparks. Miraculously, the general and his companions escaped this deadly danger. Then Jackson's luck turned bad again. Twice during the painful trip toward medical help behind the lines a stretcher bearer fell—one when shot through both arms, the second when he tripped over something in the dark woods. Both times Jackson was pitched out directly onto his mangled arm. In at least one instance the bearers were carrying the stretcher at shoulder height, presumably with the general on his back. That meant that he fell nearly six feet, turning in mid air, to land on the already shattered limb. The incredible pain that ensued caused Jackson to moan "frequently and piteously," an attendant wrote.

When Jackson at last reached his chief surgeon, waiting with an ambulance and ample medical supplies, the general hovered on the verge of death. "For two hours he was nearly pulseless," Dr. Hunter H. McGuire wrote. Jackson recognized the unspoken diagnosis: "I fear I am dying," he said calmly. Since the bleeding had not been serious at first, and yet Jackson had nearly bled to death by the time he reached the rear, the falls from the litter seem to have been the most deadly agents. The jagged bones broken by bullets probably tore open an artery during the worst of the falls.

ACROSS THE RIVER

McGuire amputated Jackson's maimed left arm early on May 3 under an ether anesthetic. The doctor was optimistic about the prospects for full recovery. Jackson rallied that morning, while the guns roared four miles away at Chancellorsville where Lee was putting the final seal on a great but bloody victory. When a trusted staff officer came to Jackson seeking advice, the wounded general's "eye flashed its old fire, but it was only for a moment; his face relaxed again, and presently he answered very feebly and sadly, 'I don't know—I can't tell...." On the 4th, a doleful cavalcade bearing the stricken lieutenant general wended its way southeastward toward Guiney Station, more than twenty-five miles distant. There Jackson could convalesce in relative safety from Federal raiders and be near the railroad, on which he might be removed to Richmond to complete his recuperation. The general's friends the Chandlers of "Fairfield," whom he had met months earlier, offered comfortable accommodations.

When McGuire rode ahead of the ambulance to prepare for the general's arrival, he found that the Chandlers had already taken several wounded soldiers into their home. Some of the casualties suffered from infections that might threaten Jackson's recovery, so McGuire fixed up a place for his patient in a small outbuilding in the yard—the plantation "office," which also had been a doctor's office before the war. The wounded warrior settled into that pleasant setting late in the evening of the 4th. During May 5 and

The Chandler family out-building in which Jackson died.

6 Jackson talked about his favorite theological subjects with staff members while his body began to recover from the trauma it had suffered. McGuire planned to move the general to Richmond by train on the 7th.

At 2 a.m. on May 7 a frightening, deadly change interrupted Jackson's recovery. Overnight the general's chest had begun to hurt badly; his lungs were affected; "his breathing was bad & gasping"; by midday, McGuire diagnosed pneumonia. (Modern doctors revel in proving to their own satisfaction that Jackson actually had something else.) At that frightening moment the patient's survival, and the prospects of the Confederate States, became problematic. Mary Anna Jackson and baby Julia reached Guiney on the ill-starred 7th. One of the first sights that awaited Anna was a coffin being exhumed in the yard. It held, she was told (a fearful omen), the body of a neighbor and friend from Lexington. The baby, "exceedingly bright and playful," crawled happily across her stricken father's bed, oblivious of the death that stalked the room. He held Julia with his remaining arm and stroked her hair. Anna helplessly watched her husband decline. Medical specialists who came up from Richmond by rail could do no more. On Sunday the 10th, Dr. McGuire told Jackson that he could not survive the day. The general responded: "Very good; very good; it is all right....My wish is fulfilled. I have always desired to die on Sunday." McGuire's forecast came true at 3:15 p.m. Jackson called in a choking, delirious, dying voice for his subordinates and whispered battle orders. Then, calmly, "Let us cross over the river, and rest under the shade of the trees."

MOURNING

"The great and good Jackson is no more," R. E. Lee wrote to J. E. B. Stuart. "He died yesterday at 3:15 p.m. of pneumonia, calm, serene, and happy. May his spirit pervade our whole army; our country will then be secure." The nation poured out its grief and worry in a succession of memorial events. A special train picked up Jackson's "very fine coffin and two large wreaths of flowers laying on it" at Guiney. Five thousand citizens met the funerary train in Richmond. The whole city lined the streets as the cortege wended its way to the capitol. Twenty thousand mourners streamed past the catafalque there, which was draped with the first sample of a brand-new national flag. "I never saw human faces show such grief—almost despair," recalled a young woman in the crowd. The funeral oration derived from Isaiah 2:22: "Cease ye from man whose breath is in his nostrils."

Stonewall's grieving countrymen lined the route his funeral procession followed to Gordonsville and Lynchburg, firing salutes and offering tributes. Other thousands attended the corpse upon its homecoming to Lexington. On May 15 the general was laid to rest there. Twenty-eight years later his remains were moved a few feet to a new setting under an imposing bronze statue. His amputated arm remains in the Wilderness, on a quiet hillside under a small marker. The house where Jackson died is preserved today and open to the public. The clock that ticked his last moments on earth stills runs in the death room, looking down on the original death bed.

"OH, FOR...'OLD JACK'"

Southerners endeavored most earnestly to convince themselves that Jackson's God would raise up someone in his stead. They were wrong. R. E. Lee quickly learned by hard experience how difficult fighting without Jackson would be. "Such an executive officer," the army commander declared, "the sun never shone on." Lee completely reorganized the army around the absence of the stalwart executor of his plans. He found at Gettysburg that none of his corps commanders was able and/or willing to accomplish his wishes crisply and cleverly. The chief of the dead lieutenant general's staff bewailed Stonewall's absence during a moment at Gettysburg that cried out for energy and determination: "Oh, for the presence and inspiration of 'Old Jack' for just one hour!"

His superb military abilities aside, the awesome impact Jackson had exerted upon both friend and foe left an unfillable Confederate vacuum and simultaneously closed a gaping psychological chink in Unionist armor. Joshua Howell of the 47th Alabama wrote to his wife four days after Jackson died that as a consequence of the disaster, "I think the north will whip us soon." Mississippian Howard McCaleb ruefully declared the loss to be "irreparable....We all felt that a heavy stone of sorrow had been rolled upon our hearts." Sidney Jackson of the 21st Georgia wrote on May 12, "if we could only see Jackson, we was all right....He was thought more of then are nother [any other] general that we have got."

George Washington Miley of the 10th Virginia Infantry worried about improved Union morale with Jackson gone. The enemy will "have more daring when they consider our weighty loss," he wrote on May 13. "They know that such a warrior as Jackson will be hard to find, and [even] if his place can be filled by one who is his equal, they will still have to learn to fear him, before his name will be a terror to them." Miley was exactly right, but he might have been surprised by the volume of warm comment about Jackson in the North. Union Surgeon J. H. Brinton noticed that the demise of the famous enemy leader caused "no elation in our army. All recognized [Jackson as] honorable and brave...a military genius....The feeling of the Northern army was one of pity, I might also say of regret, that so great a soldier was passing away." A New York artillerist wrote, "I do not feel like exulting over the grave of such a brave, wise, and energetic antagonist." Northern generals exhibited similar sentiments. Abraham Lincoln congratulated a Washington editor for the "excellent and manly" nature of a warm tribute to Jackson printed on May 13. Jacobins wielding petty power often showed less tolerance: a number of Federals were convicted by courts martial for saying nice things about Jackson, or proposing toasts to his health. Such jingoism subsided steadily in the aftermath of war. Within a few decades, Jackson had become virtually as great a hero in the North as in the South. He remains today one of the most compelling figures in the most fascinating of the country's historical eras.

AFTERWORD

Stonewall Jackson's standing in America's military pantheon—a large niche, in the front rank—had been assured by the time of his death. Precisely how his countrymen would view him has of course been affected by the passage of time and the accumulation of legends of mythic proportions. Within weeks of the general's death, biographies began to pour off presses and into the hands of avidly curious readers. The Confederate-imprint versions of those biographies remain today very attractive to collectors, albeit decidedly expensive. New York houses shamelessly pirated Southern biographies, secure in the knowledge that Rebels had no recourse to copyright courts. Before May 1863 ended, two prominent officers running for a seat in the Confederate Congress were sparring in public over the salient issue in their race: which of them would the dead Jackson endorse, were he still alive? Southern preachers hymned the life, religious character, and death of the martyred hero far more frequently than they focused on the Sermon on the Mount. When Jackson's favorite preacher essayed the subject in an army camp, so many men climbed on the chapel roof that it collapsed, crushing several of them. A Georgian major who survived said of the three-hour sermon, "I have never heard anything more sublime, nor had anything to make so great an impression in my life." A Mississippian listening to the eulogy noticed "tears coursing down the cheek from many a manly eye."[68]

Europeans, especially the English, who had observed the war from afar were fascinated with Jackson and eager to learn more of him. London-imprint biographies (and one issued in Halifax, Nova Scotia, too) appeared almost as soon as those from Richmond presses, and were read with as much interest. The London *Times* declared on May 27: "on this side of the ocean the gallant soldier's fate will everywhere be heard of with pity and sympathy, not only as a brave man fighting for his country's independence, but as one of the consumate generals that this century has produced." The London *Evening Standard* exclaimed: "he was a hero after our own heart, one of those men whose gallantry and virtues shed imperishable luster over the cause they embrace."

A Southern poet prophesied aptly in late 1862: "And men shall tell their children/ Tho' all other memories fade/ That they fought with *Stonewall Jackson*/ In the old 'Stonewall Brigade!'" A Louisianian under Jackson, although not in the brigade itself, told his wife, "I had rather be a private in such an army than a field officer in any other army. Jackson is perfectly idolized." Not long after Jackson's death men who had never been anywhere near him began to claim the chance to bask in his reflected glow. During August 1864, citizens Peter Manley and Francis Labruge of Missouri came before unrelated courts martial and claimed with obvious pride that they had fought under Stonewall Jackson at Vicksburg and at Hannibal, Missouri. Neither had ever been within hundreds of miles of the dead hero, but the itch for association with his luminous legend was irresistible. Thousands more made the same switch to Jackson's standard as "all other memories fade[d]." By 1870 half of them believed the story themselves; by 1890 all of them did. To this day, a great many descendants who approach Civil War historians looking for help finding traces of their ancestors bear family lore about "fighting under Stonewall Jackson"—even if their 1860's soldier had served his time in Missouri orTexas or Arkansas or (especially) in Longstreet's Corps.[69]

Almost at once, Jackson's hagiographic image in Southern print came to be reflected by Northern biographers, whose readers had been fond of the legend from the start. For three decades after the war little that was new, serious, or important was added to the literature on Jackson. The great military biography by English Colonel George F. R. Henderson (still, after 100 years, the best military analysis of the general) that appeared near the end of the century was generally judicious, but came down squarely on Jackson's side in every instance—including some special pleading about the Seven Days failures. No one of note levelled any serious, basic criticisms against Jackson until the modern age of the anti-hero. Revisionists eager to spit against the tide for the sheer ecstacy of being noticed have undertaken assaults on all Confederate legends, including Jackson. One ponderous study claimed to demonstrate that Southerners knew they *ought* to lose, and subconsciously wanted to, and made sure that they did; this profundity was denominated "cognitive dissonance." A great deal of current academic writing about the Confederacy elaborates this fatuous notion. Better balanced military studies have reflected analytically on turning points and options open to Jackson, from which other military results might have ensued. Much recent scholarship has examined his battles in searching detail.

It is inconceivable that Americans at the end of the 21st (and 25th) century will be anything but fascinated by the pious, stern, enigmatic, determined Stonewall Jackson, who has captivated the imagination of every generation since the time he earned this country's most famous *nom de guerre* nearly 140 years ago.

Reader's Note: The footnotes and the complete bibliography to this work have been placed on file for viewing purposes at the Gettysburg National Military Park library. Readers may obtain a set of footnotes and the complete bibliography by sending $2.00 to the Farnsworth House Book Shop, 401 Baltimore Street, Gettysburg, PA 17325.

SELECT BIBLIOGRAPHY

Arnold, Thomas Jackson. *Early Life and Letters of General Thomas J. Jackson*. New York: Fleming H. Revell Company, 1916.

Chambers, Lenoir. *Stonewall Jackson*. New York: William Morrow & Company, 1959. 2 vols.

Chase, William C. *Story of Stonewall Jackson*. Atlanta: D.E. Luther Pub. Co., 1901.

Chew, R.P. *Stonewall Jackson*. Lexington, Virginia: Rockbridge County News Print, 1912.

Clopton, J.J. *The True Stonewall Jackson*. Baltimore: Ruths' Sons, Printers, 1913.

Cook, Roy Bird. *The Family and Early Life of Stonewall Jackson*. Richmond: Old Dominion Press, 1924.

Cooke, John Esten. *The Life of Stonewall Jackson*. Richmond: Ayres & Wade, 1863.

__________. *Stonewall Jackson, A Military Biography*. New York: D. Appleton and Co., 1876.

Coulling, Mary P. *Margaret Junkin Preston*. Winston-Salem, North Carolina: John F. Blair, 1993.

Dabney, Robert L. *Life and Campaigns of Liet.-Gen. Thomas J. Jackson*. New York: Blelock & Co., 1866.

Daniel, John Warwick. *Character of Stonewall Jackson*. Lynchburg, Virginia: Schaffter & Bryant, Printers, 1868.

Graham, Henry Tucker. *Stonewall Jackson*. Florence, South Carolina, n.d.

Hallock, Charles. *A Complete Biographical Sketch of "Stonewall" Jackson*. Augusta, Georgia: Steam Power Press Chronicle and Sentinel, 1863.

Henderson, George F.R. Stonewall Jackson and the American Civil War. 2 vols. London: Longmans, Green, and Co., 1898.

Hopley, Catherine C. *"Stonewall" Jackson, Late General of the Confederate States Army*. London: Chapman and Hall, 1863.

Jackson, Mary Anna Morrison. *Life and Letters of General Thomas J. Jackson*. New York: Harper & Brothers, 1892.

____________. *Memoirs of Stonewall Jackson*. Louisville, Kentucky: The Prentice Press, 1895.

Junkin, Margaret. *Silverwood: A Book of Memories*. New York: Irby & Jackson, 1856.

McCabe, James D. *The Life of Thomas J. Jackson*. Richmond: James E. Goode, 1864.

McGuire, Hunter Holmes. *Stonewall Jackson, an Address*. Richmond, 1897.

Randolph, Sarah Nicholas. *The Life of Gen. Thomas J. Jackson*. Philadelphia: J.B. Lippincott & Co., 1876.

Riley, Elihu S. *"Stonewall Jackson"*. Annapolis, Maryland, 1920.

Robertson, James I., Jr. *Stonewall Jackson*. New York: McGraw-Hill Book Co., 1957.

Smith, Francis Henney. *Discourse on the Life and Character of Lt. Gen. Thos. J. Jackson*. Richmond: Ritchie & Dunnavant, Printers, 1863.

Tate, Allen. *Stonewall Jackson, the Good Soldier*. New York: Minton Balch & Co., 1928.

Vandiver, Frank E. *Mighty Stonewall*. New York: McGraw-Hill Book Co., 1957.

Wayland, John W. *Stonewall Jackson's Way*. Staunton, Virginia: McClure Co., 1940.

Author Robert K. Krick grew up in California and earned degrees from Pacific Union College and San Jose State University. He has lived and worked on east-coast battlefields for more than thirty years. Krick has written ten books and more than one hundred published articles. His *Stonewall Jackson at Cedar Mountain* (University of North Carolina Press, 1990) won three national prizes, including the Douglas Southall Freeman Award. Both *Stonewall Jackson at Cedar Mountain* and *Lee's Colonels* (Morningside, 1992, fourth edition) were selections of the History Book Club. Krick's latest book, *Conquering the Valley: Stonewall Jackson at Port Republic* (William Morrow, 1996), was a main selection of the History Book Club and a selection of the Book-of-the-Month Club. He is proud of his role as a founder of the Central Virginia Battlefields Trust, which is hard at work in defense of that region's dwindling Civil War heritage.

FARNSWORTH HOUSE PUBLICATIONS

"TRUST IN GOD AND FEAR NOTHING" GENERAL LEWIS A. ARMISTEAD, CSA, by Wayne E. Motts, w/afterword by Lewis B. Armistead. Farnsworth House Civil War Commander Series #1.

"THE DEVIL'S TO PAY" GENERAL JOHN BUFORD, USA, by Michael Phipps and John Peterson, w/afterword by Senator Tom Buford. Farnsworth House Commander Series #2.

"FAITHFULLY AND FOREVER YOUR SOLDIER" GENERAL GEORGE E. PICKETT, CSA, by Richard F. Selcer, w/ afterword by George E. Pickett. Farnsworth House Commander Series #3.

"FOR GOD'S SAKE FORWARD" GENERAL JOHN F. REYNOLDS, USA, by Michael A. Riley, afterword by Alan T. Nolan. Farnsworth House Commander Series #4.

"COME ON YOU WOLVERINES!" CUSTER AT GETTYSBURG, by Michael Phipps, w/afterword by Paul Andrew Hutton. Commander Series #5.

"DUTY FAITHFULLY PERFORMED" GENERAL ROBERT E. LEE, CSA, by Gary W. Gallagher. Farnsworth House Commander Series #6.

TRAVELLER & COMPANY: THE HORSES OF GETTYSBURG, by Blake A. Magner, w/foreword by Mark Meyers.

THE BATTLE OF GETTYSBURG, by Major General George Gordon Meade. (Self contained extract from General Meade's Life and Letters, edited by his son).

KELLY'S HEROES: THE IRISH BRIGADE AT GETTYSBURG, by T. L. Murphy.